Mutual Funds
Boost Your Wealth with Time-Tested Investment Vehicles

Table of Contents

Chapter 1. Introduction

Welcome to a special report that has your financial future at its heart – "Mutual Funds: Boost Your Wealth with Time-Tested Investment Vehicles." Embarking on a financial journey can be daunting, yet incredibly rewarding. This comprehensive guide aims to enlighten you about the time-honored, dynamic world of mutual funds. We promise this is not an arcane math paper filled with complex formulas. Instead, we break down the essence of mutual funds into easily digestible portions, using straightforward language peppered with real-life examples. A smorgasbord of empowerment and knowledge lies within these pages, ready to reveal the elusive secrets of wealth multiplication. So, whether you're a novice dipping your toes into the investment waters or a seasoned investor aiming to expand your horizons, this special report is tailored for you. Prepare to leverage the power of time and compounding in your journey towards realizing your financial dreams by understanding the long-serving vehicle of mutual funds. Let's take that first step together, starting right here, right now!

Chapter 2. Understanding Mutual Funds: Basic Concepts and Definitions

Mutual funds are complex yet attractive vehicles for investment, offering a plethora of opportunities to those who understand their fundamental concepts and mechanisms. At the root of it all, they are simply an aggregation of funds from multiple investors, managed professionally with the goal of income or capital gains. However, there's much more to digest before you can gain full comprehension of these vehicles.

2.1. The Origin of Mutual Funds

The journey of mutual funds as an investment instrument started back in 1774, in the Netherlands. But the first modern mutual fund, as we recognize it today, was established in 1924 in Boston, United States. Initially, they were considered a vehicle for the wealthy, but the inception of mass-market funds in the 1970s transformed mutual funds into an accessible investment option for the general public.

2.2. Understanding the structure

A mutual fund typically has three key entities: the fund's investors, the fund manager, and the fund's trustee. Investors contribute money into the fund, which the fund manager (also known as Asset Management Company or AMC) uses to invest in various securities, as per the guidelines of the fund. The fund's trustee overlooks operations to ensure regulation compliance. This structure not only maintains transparency but also allows for a division of responsibilities, ensuring that the fund's operations are run smoothly and professionally.

A mutual fund can be either open-ended or close-ended. Close-ended funds have a fixed maturity period and their units are initially offered through an IPO before trading begins on the stock market. Open-ended funds, on the other hand, have no fixed maturity period and investors can purchase or redeem their units at any time. This distinction can greatly affect the liquidity and pricing of the fund's units.

2.3. Understanding various types of funds

Mutual funds can be classified based on their investment objective, structuring, and mode of operation. The following are some of the most common types you'll likely come across during your investment journey:

1. Equity Funds: These mutual funds invest predominantly in stocks. They offer the potential for high returns, but also come with higher risk.

2. Debt Funds: These funds invest in fixed income securities like bonds and treasury bills. They offer more stability and are less risky, but with proportionately lower returns.

3. Balanced or Hybrid Funds: These funds invest in a mix of equity and debt, balancing the risk and rewards.

4. Sector Funds: These funds invest specifically in one sector, like IT, pharmaceuticals, real estate etc. Their performance is reliant on the performance of the associated sector.

5. Index Funds: Such funds track specific indices like the S&P 500 or Sensex, aiming to replicate their performance.

6. Fund of Funds: These funds invest in other mutual funds, hence offering greater diversification.

Understanding your own risk appetite, financial goals, and time constraints is crucial before deciding which type of fund best suits your needs.

2.4. Breakdown of Mutual Fund Costs

Investing in mutual funds isn't free. It's important to understand the different types of costs involved with these investments:

1. Expense Ratio: This is the annual fee that all funds charge their shareholders. It represents the percentage of assets dedicated to running the fund.

2. Load: This is the sales charge or commission applied when buying or selling a mutual fund. However, 'No-load' funds do not charge this fee.

3. Management Fee: This forms part of the Expense Ratio and is paid to the fund manager for their services.

4. Redemption Fee: This is a fee charged for withdrawals from a fund within a particular timeframe. This timeframe is usually noted in the fund's prospectus.

5. Account Fees: Certain funds might charge annual maintenance costs, especially for accounts with balances less than the defined minimum.

Understanding these costs aids in comparing different funds, developing investment strategies, and calculating net returns on your investments.

By now, you should have a baseline knowledge about the basic concepts and definitions involving mutual funds. Armed with this information, you're on your way to navigate your financial journey confidently and profitably. In the next chapter, we'll shed light on the underpinnings of mutual fund operations, risk considerations, and how to be mindful of market fluctuations. Stay tuned and join us in the next stage of this enlightening journey.

Chapter 3. The Power of Compounding: Enhancing Wealth Over Time

In the world of finance, nothing probably holds such a profound impact as the principle of compounding. It is a deceptively simple concept, but its repercussions are far-reaching. Compounding forms the backbone of long-term wealth creation. By reaping the twin benefits of time and repeatedly earned interest, it exponentially amplifies your wealth.

3.1. The Basics of Compounding

Compounding is the process by which an investment grows over time as the earnings it generates are reinvested. This creates a snowball effect, where a little bit of snow rolling down a hill becomes much larger over time. In the context of an investment, especially in mutual funds, the dividends or interest received are reinvested back, producing greater returns over the years.

An important aspect to understand here is that compounding returns aren't linear but exponential. This means that rather than growing in a simple, step-by-step manner, returns accelerate over time, creating a curve that becomes steeper as time progresses.

3.2. The Magic of Compound Interest

Historically, Albert Einstein has been attributed with the quote: "Compound interest is the eighth wonder of the world. He who understands it, earns it; he who doesn't, pays it." Despite this attribution being disputed, the quote resonates deeply as the reality of compounding is stunningly effective.

Interest on interest – that's the basic premise of compound interest. It sounds deceptively simple, doesn't it? However, the results it yields over a prolonged period can be mind-blowing.

To understand the concept of compound interest, let's consider a simple example. If you invest $10,000 at an annual interest rate of 5%, at the end of the first year, you will have $10,500 ($10,000 plus $500 interest). If you leave that money in the investment, you don't just earn interest on the initial $10,000 in the second year. Instead, you earn it on the new total of $10,500. That may not seem like a major difference after just one year, but over the course of several years, that extra compounding significantly adds up.

3.3. The Time Factor

Time plays a crucial role in the magic of compounding. The earlier you start investing, the more time your investment has to grow. Each year's returns build off of the previous years' – it's the snowball effect again.

While investment performance can never be guaranteed, the mathematics of compounding remains constant, regardless of the investment environment. The longer you leave your money with compounding investments, the greater the likelihood of enhanced returns.

Arthur, who starts investing at age 25, will significantly outperform Bob, who begins at 35 – even if Bob invests more money. This exemplifies the time aspect in power of compounding.

3.4. Regular investments

Regular investments or systematic investment plans (SIPs) can significantly augment the power of compounding. Through SIPs, you invest a fixed amount in a mutual fund scheme at regular intervals. The consistent investments at different market levels ensure more units when prices are low and fewer units when prices are high, leading to cost averaging over time.

3.5. The Rule of 72

To understand how compounding works and how quickly your money will double, consider the rule of 72. Simply divide 72 by your rate of return to estimate the number of years it will take for your investment to double in value.

3.6. Compounding in Mutual Funds

Mutual funds are particularly popular because they compound daily, not annually. Therefore, every day your earnings have the potential to earn more for you. Distributed dividends and capital gains can automatically be reinvested to buy more shares, thereby growing your fund even further.

3.7. Conclusion

The power of compounding is not just about enhancing wealth over time, but it is also about developing financial disciplines such as regular investing and long-term outlook. The magic of compounding comes alive only when given time. The earlier and longer you invest, the more you can reap the benefits of compounding. Understand this, and you unlock a powerful tool in your financial toolkit. As with most good things in life, the key ingredient here is patience. Be patient, remain invested, and watch your wealth grow over time.

Chapter 4. Types of Mutual Funds: Picking the Best Fit for Your Financial Goals

Starting your journey towards financial literacy, the very first step is to comprehend the types of mutual funds available. Mutual funds are diversified, pre-constructed portfolios of stocks, bonds, or other securities, which can save you an enormous amount of time and money compared to buying a myriad of individual securities. However, the mutual fund universe is vast and varied. Let's begin exploring the most predominant kinds.

4.1. Money Market Funds

Money market funds invest in short-term, high-quality fixed-income securities. These include treasury bills (T-bills), certificates of deposit (CDs), and commercial paper. Because of their conservative nature, money market funds are considered one of the lowest-risk types of mutual funds. They aim to maintain a net asset value (NAV) of $1 per share, making them a favorite choice for conservative investors.

Investors often use money market funds as a substitute for checking or savings accounts, given their relatively higher returns. However, they're not FDIC-insured, meaning they still carry some level of risk.

4.2. Equity Funds

Equity funds, also known as stock funds, represent the largest category of mutual funds. As the name suggests, these funds invest primarily in stocks. There are numerous sub-types of equity funds, categorized by company size (large-cap, mid-cap, small-cap), investment style (growth, value, blend), or geographical focus (domestic, international, emerging markets).

These funds offer the highest potential returns among all types of mutual funds. However, they also come with higher risk because stock prices are very volatile. If you're an aggressive investor with a long-term outlook, equity funds could be a key component of your portfolio.

4.3. Fixed Income Funds

Fixed income funds invest primarily in bonds and other debt securities with the aim to provide regular income to investors. These funds can be a good option for conservative investors seeking a steady income stream. They're also beneficial for retirees, who can use the income as part of their withdrawal strategy.

Fixed income funds can invest in various types of bonds, including corporate bonds, government bonds, or municipal bonds. The level of risk and income potential depend significantly on the type of bonds in which the fund invests.

4.4. Balanced Funds

Balanced funds, or hybrid funds, invest in a mix of stocks, bonds, and other securities. They aim to strike a balance between the growth potential of stocks and the income stability of bonds, allowing investors to pursue growth while maintaining some income.

Typically, balanced funds maintain a particular ratio of stocks to bonds. A "70/30" fund, for example, would keep 70% of its total assets in stocks and 30% in bonds. This ratio, however, can vary based on the fund's objective and the fund manager's philosophy.

4.5. Index Funds

Index funds seek to replicate the performance of a specific index, such as the S&P 500. These are passively managed funds, meaning that the fund manager does not actively buy and sell securities within the fund. Instead, the fund simply holds the same securities as the underlying index.

This type of mutual fund is favored by investors who believe in market efficiency, i.e., that all current information is already reflected in stock prices, and it's challenging to outperform the market. Index funds offer minimal transaction costs, low management fees, and broad market exposure.

4.6. Sector Funds

Sector funds focus on specific sectors of the economy, such as technology, healthcare, or energy. This focus allows for concentrated growth potential but also brings increased risk. A downturn in the specific sector can lead to significant losses for the fund.

These funds are best for investors who want to take advantage of the booming performance of a particular sector. However, they require thorough understanding and constant monitoring of the sector in question.

4.7. International & Global Funds

International funds invest in non-US companies, while global funds invest in a combination of US and non-US companies. These funds offer diversification outside the domestic market, which can help reduce risk.

However, investing outside your home country can introduce new challenges, including currency fluctuations and geopolitical risks.

Adequate research should be undertaken before investing in these types of mutual funds.

4.8. Commodity Funds

Commodity funds invest in physical commodities, like gold, silver, oil, or agricultural products. They offer a hedge against inflation as commodities usually increase in price when the cost of living rises.

However, these funds are considered high-risk and are best suited for experienced investors who understand the volatility and risks associated with commodities.

4.9. Funds of Funds

Funds of Funds (FoFs) take diversification a step further by investing in multiple mutual funds, rather than individual securities. They offer diversification among various asset classes and investment styles, providing a "one-stop" investment solution.

Yet, this broad diversification comes at a cost. FoFs have higher expense ratios due to the double layer of fees - management fees of the FoF itself, plus the fees of the underlying funds.

Now that we've looked into the prevailing types of mutual funds, it's clear that there's no one-size-fits-all solution when it comes to investing. Your individual financial goals, risk tolerance, and investment horizon should dictate your choice of mutual fund. Understanding these types of mutual funds will help you make an informed choice, aligning your investment strategy with your unique financial goals. Thus, with knowledge and time on your side, you are now well-equipped to embarking successfully on your investment journey.

Chapter 5. Mutual Funds vs. Other Investment Vehicles: A Comparative Analysis

Investing can often resemble a complex game of chess, where every move can lead to numerous potential outcomes, each vastly different from the other. As challenging as this game may seem, knowledge about your potential moves i.e., investment options, can steer you towards profit and away from losses.

Comparing mutual funds with other investment vehicles is an effective strategy to broaden the understanding of the investment arena, one where the former has carved a niche owing to embedded advantages such as diversification and professional management. However, that's not to say other investment vehicles lack merits.

Investing solely in mutual funds or other investment vehicles should not be your focus. Instead, it should be about understanding each of them, knowing when and where they do well and utilizing this knowledge to construct a well-rounded portfolio. Let's begin our exploration.

5.1. Equities (Individual Stocks)

An individual stock is an equity security representing a proportional share of ownership in a company. Hence, purchasing individual stocks leads to partial ownership of the firm.

The highlight of individual stocks is the massive potential for returns. A right pick can see your invested capital multiply many times over a short period. But, it's not devoid of risks.

When you invest in a single company, you are exposed to unique risks associated with that entity. If the company underperforms or goes bankrupt, you risk losing a substantial part, if not all, of your investment.

Comparatively, mutual funds are less risky as they invest in a diversified portfolio of many companies across sectors. You do not have the danger of your investment spiralling down to zero, unlike in the case of individual stocks.

Managing individual stocks demands time, skill, and dedication. You need to track markets and company news, analyze reports, predict trends and make buying, holding or selling decisions. In contrast, mutual funds come with a fund manager who does all these tasks for you. Thus, mutual funds can be considered more convenient than individual stocks.

It's essential to note that direct equities can offer you greater control over your investments than mutual funds. You get to determine which companies you invest in and when you want to buy or sell.

5.2. Bonds and Fixed-Income Securities

Bonds or fixed-income securities are debt instruments that companies or governments issue to raise funds. As an investor, you essentially lend your money in exchange for periodic interest payments and the return of principal at maturity.

Bonds are generally considered safer than equity investments but yield smaller returns compared to stocks. They offer a predictable stream of income, making them suitable for conservative investors seeking capital preservation.

In comparison, mutual funds can offer the potential for higher returns, especially those eyeing the long-term horizon with a portfolio tilted towards equities.

Mutual funds also invest in bonds; thus, investors can benefit from the safety of bonds through debt mutual funds.

However, investing in individual bonds is not as liquid as mutual funds as the former can be hard to sell, especially in a thin market. In contrast, you can easily buy and sell mutual fund units on any business day, providing greater liquidity.

5.3. Real Estate

Real estate is another popular route investors take. Like equities, investing in real estate allows you to own a physical asset, offering potential profits through rental income and capital appreciation.

The main difference versus mutual funds lies in the tangibility – real estate is a physical asset, whereas mutual funds represent a share in a diversified portfolio. Additionally, the ticket size for real estate is significantly higher than that for mutual funds, which restricts its accessibility.

Investing in real estate requires substantial management effort – from maintenance and dealing with tenants to understanding local real estate laws. Mutual Funds, on the other hand, are managed by fund managers, making it an entirely passive investment.

However, if your preference leans towards owning a physical asset while earning periodic income and hoping for long-term capital appreciation, real estate may be worth considering.

5.4. Conclusion

As we can see, each investment vehicle has its advantages and disadvantages, and no one-size-fits-all approach works.

Mutual funds provide exposure to a diversified portfolio, risk mitigation, professional management, and lower investment minimums. On the other hand, individual stocks offer high potential returns, greater control over investments and ownership rights. Bonds promise predictable income and safety, but at the expense of liquidity and potentially lower returns. Real estate provides tangible assets, high value, and rental income but is marred by higher entry barriers and extensive management.

Your investment decision should depend on your financial goals, risk tolerance, investment horizon, and convenience. Do not shy away from consulting a financial advisor to better understand these nuances and align your investments with your financial goals.

Remember, each of these investment vehicles offers a vehicle to travel along the road to financial independence; you just have to choose the one that best fits your route. By understanding how these options differ and where they align, you unlock the ability to build a portfolio that serves your needs today and evolves as those needs change over time.

Chapter 6. The Risk-Reward Balance: How Mutual Funds Fit into Your Portfolio

To comprehend the value mutual funds carry for your portfolio, one must first grasp the intricate dance between risk and reward in the investing arena. Venturing into this world entails embarking on a journey filled with possible pitfalls and gains alike. In this context, we'll dissect the essential aspects of the aforementioned balance, illuminating how mutual funds may function as a weighting scale in your investment portfolio.

6.1. Establishing your Risk Profile

Before you pour your hard-earned money into any investment, it is important to understand your risk profile. This is essentially a measure of your ability and willingness to bear losses in exchange for potential higher returns. It varies greatly among individuals and hinges upon factors such as age, income, financial goals, liabilities, and psychological factors that may mold an investor's propensity towards risk-taking.

Examining these aspects can tell you whether you're a conservative, moderate, or aggressive investor. A conservative (or low risk-tolerance) investor is likely to prioritize capital preservation over high returns. These individuals typically lean towards secure, low-risk investments and are willing to accept lower returns for the peace of mind that their original sum will remain intact.

Moderate investors are willing to experience some volatility for potential future growth. They carefully balance the weight of risk and reward, leaning neither too excessively towards preservation nor profit.

Aggressive investors, or those with high-risk tolerance, prioritize high returns even if it entails substantial risk. These individuals might be comfortable with investments that promise high returns but also carry a chance of capital loss.

6.2. How Mutual Funds Offset Risks

Navigating this risk-reward spectrum, mutual funds offer a middle ground, serving as an essential tool for diversification. They pool resources from multiple investors to invest in a variety of instruments such as stocks, bonds, money market instruments, and more, spreading out the investment risk.

This diversified investment approach has two significant advantages. First, it enables individual investors to hold a small part of a broad range of investments, providing exposure to different sectors, companies, and asset classes. Second, it helps minimize the impact of a poor-performing asset on the entire portfolio, as not all your investments are tied up in one basket.

Over lime, the diversification effect of mutual funds can result in more stable returns. Of course, mutual funds carry risk, but because they are spread over multiple investment assets, they can manage and mitigate these risks more effectively.

6.3. Balance of Active and Passive Investments

Mutual funds are also a blend of passive and active investment styles. Passive mutual funds, such as index funds, try to mimic the performance of a specific benchmark or index. They provide broad market exposure, low portfolio turnover, and low operating expenses.

On the other hand, actively managed mutual funds have fund

managers making specific investment decisions in an attempt to outperform an index. While these may offer the potential for higher returns, they also carry higher risk and generally have higher expense ratios due to increased management activity.

The balance here is that a portfolio can benefit both from the stability provided by passive investments and the potential upside from active picks. Depending on risk appetite and expectations, one may tilt more towards one than the other.

6.4. Types of Mutual Funds and Risk-Reward Dynamics

There's a wide array of mutual funds available, each with its own risk-reward dynamics. For instance, equity or stock funds come with the potential for high returns and high risks as they invest in company shares. On the other hand, debt funds invest in fixed income securities like government and corporate bonds, offering lower risk and steady returns.

Balanced or hybrid funds provide a mix of equity and debt, both mitigating risk and potentially offering decent returns. Sector funds focus on specific sectors, which can offer high rewards but are proportionally risky due to a lack of diversification. Lastly, index funds and ETFs offer a broad market exposure and follow a passive strategy, serving as relatively low risk investment options.

Understanding these dynamics can guide you on where to place mutual funds within your portfolio and how to use them to achieve your financial goals.

6.5. Allocating Mutual Funds for your Financial Objectives

Each investor has unique financial goals, whether it's saving for retirement, a child's education, a dream vacation, or a down payment for a house. One's success largely depends on identifying these goals, establishing timelines, and choosing the right mutual funds that fit well within one's risk tolerance and expected returns framework.

Short-term goals might lead you towards debt or money market funds with less risk and more immediate returns. On the other hand, for long-term goals, you might want to consider equity funds that come with greater risk but offer higher potential rewards over time.

Remember, while mutual funds offer a myriad of advantages, they are not devoid of risks. But with an understanding of your risk tolerance and financial objectives teamed with an effective diversification strategy, they can act as a powerful tool in the journey to achieving your financial dreams. Remember, investing is not a one-size-fits-all approach. The key lies in astute planning, consistent investments, review, and rebalancing as required.

Chapter 7. Reading a Mutual Fund Prospectus: Your Guide to Making Informed Decisions

Embarking on your journey towards investing in mutual funds, it is crucial to thoroughly comprehend the fund prospectus. A prospectus is a legally mandated document that provides detailed information about a particular fund. Reading through a prospectus might seem daunting, but it's fairly manageable when broken down into its essential parts.

7.1. What is a Mutual Fund Prospectus?

A mutual fund prospectus is a comprehensive document that fund companies are obligated to issue. It unveils key details of a mutual fund's investment objectives, strategies, risks, costs, and past performance. The plethora of information imparted through a mutual fund prospectus is meant to help investors make informed decisions. Remember that fund companies often issue more user-friendly, summarized versions of the prospectus. However, only the full prospectus carries all the essential and minute details.

7.2. How to Read a Mutual Fund Prospectus?

The prospectus is broken down into sections, each detailing specifics about the fund's operations, strategies, and potential risks.

7.2.1. Investment Objectives

Getting clarity on the mutual fund's objectives is the cornerstone of any investment decision. This section illustrates the fund's financial goal, for example, to generate income, preserve principal, or accumulate wealth over a long period. Your financial goals should align with those of your chosen mutual fund.

7.2.2. Strategies and Types of Investments

This segment reveals how the fund plans to reach its objectives, expressing the investment strategies that it uses. For instance, a fund might focus solely on investing in bonds, equities, or commodities. Understanding whether the fund uses complex strategies, such as heavy use of derivatives or short-selling tactics, is crucial.

7.2.3. Risks

Every investment bears a degree of risk, and mutual funds are no exception. The risk section elucidates the specific risks associated with the fund's investments. These may include market risk, interest rate risk, credit risk, and liquidity risk, among others. Weigh these risks against your personal risk-tolerance levels.

7.2.4. Fees and Expenses

Investing in a mutual fund isn't free. The prospectus elaborates on the costs associated with the fund. These include management fees, distribution fees, and other expenses. This section might also include an expense example that demonstrates the potential costs over time.

7.2.5. Past Performance

While past performance cannot predict future returns, it can aid investors in understanding a fund's historical volatility. Check how the fund has fared over different time frames, such as one, five, or ten years. Make sure to compare its historical returns with its benchmark index.

7.2.6. The Fund's Management

This section reveals who manages the fund. More impressively, it unveils the manager's investment experience and possibly the performance of other funds that they manage.

7.2.7. Shareholder Information

Here, you can learn about the mechanics of investing in the fund: how to buy shares, the minimum investment requirement, how to sell shares, and the specifics of dividend distribution.

7.3. Importance of Reading a Mutual Fund Prospectus

Understanding the content of a prospectus can make the difference between a well-informed investment decision and a misinformed one. Not all mutual funds are equal, and it's important to understand the unique aspects of each one to align it with your investment strategy, risk tolerance, and financial goals.

7.4. Navigating the Fine Print

Each mutual fund prospectus contains a wealth of information, most of which is delivered in fine print. Don't overlook these subtle details – this is where you'll uncover the most crucial information, frequently tucked away in complex legalese.

7.4.1. Glossary

An essential part of the prospectus that disentangles the complexities of finance jargon. Becoming conversant with these terms can enhance your comprehension of the mutual fund's intricacies.

7.4.2. Footnotes

Footnotes often carry disclosures that can reveal essential insights about the fund, including aspects of its operation that may not be immediately apparent in the main text of the document.

7.4.3. Charts and Diagrams

Visual cues, such as charts, diagrams, or infographics, are meant to unearth complex information in a comprehensive way. They could depict the fund's historical performance, allocation of assets, or risk-return profile.

Reading a mutual fund prospectus is a time-consuming yet essential task. It's an investor's homework before committing to any investment. Therefore, having a solid understanding of its contents is pivotal not just to make an informed decision but also to keep up with your fund's performance and strategy. It's this understanding that steers your financial voyage towards your desired direction, helping you reach your long-term financial objectives. So, happy reading, and here's to a future of successful investing!

Chapter 8. The Fees and Costs Associated with Mutual Funds: A Transparent View

Like any investment instrument, mutual funds come with their unique array of fees and costs. Understanding these charges deeply not only helps us get acquainted with the nitty-gritty of mutual funds but also renders us the competence of comparing funds to make informed investment decisions. These costs effectively impact the net returns that trickle down to us, the investors. Hence, thorough comprehension is paramount. Let's shed some light on the workings of different charges associated with mutual funds.

8.1. The Expense Ratio

A vital cost attached to mutual funds is the expense ratio. It's a fee that the mutual fund company charges its investors for managing the fund. To be more specific, the expense ratio is the percentage of the fund's total asset that goes towards operational expenses, including management fee and administrative costs, among other miscellaneous expenses.

The expense ratio is calculated annually and is deducted directly from the fund's assets, which means it reduces the return investors get from the fund. Hence, a lower expense ratio is generally advantageous for investors, although other factors should be taken into consideration before making an investment decision.

For instance, Fund A might have an expense ratio of 1.5% while Fund B has an expense ratio of 0.5%. If both funds perform identically before expenses, those invested in Fund B would take home higher returns due to its lower expense ratio.

8.2. Load Fees

Apart from the expense ratio, mutual funds might be subject to load fees. Load fees are commissions charged at the time of purchasing or selling the fund, generally as a percentage of the transaction amount. They are categorized as front-end loads (charged at the time of purchase) and back-end loads (charged at the time of sale).

If you invest in a fund with a front-end load of 5%, and you contribute $10,000, you will be charged $500 upfront, and the remaining $9,500 will be invested in the fund. Similarly, a back-end load is a fee charged upon selling units of the fund. The amount is determined by the value of the shares being sold and often decreases the longer you hold the investment.

Load fees are beneficial for the mutual fund companies as they discourage short-term trading, which can be disruptive to their investment strategies. However, not all mutual funds charge load fees, and load-free funds are known as no-load funds.

8.3. 12b-1 Fees

Another common fee associated with mutual funds is the 12b-1 fee. Named after the SEC rule that permits its use, the 12b-1 fee is essentially an annual marketing or distribution fee on a mutual fund. This charge goes towards promoting the mutual fund, printing promotional materials and prospectuses, and compensating intermediaries who distribute fund shares.

The 12b-1 fee, while typically bundled into the expense ratio, is worth noting on its own, as it directly impacts the profits returned to investors. Note that this fee must be disclosed in the prospectus's fee table, all thanks to the transparency mandates by the SEC.

8.4. Redemption Fee

Certain mutual funds charge a redemption fee if you sell your shares in the fund within a certain period after purchasing them, typically within 30 to 180 days. This fee is employed to deter short-term trading in long-term investment vehicles.

The redemption fee, calculated as a percentage of the sale proceeds, is paid back into the fund's assets, not to the fund provider. This practice benefits the funds remaining shareholders by discouraging disruptive, short-term trades which could potentially impact the fund's overall performance.

8.5. Account Fees

Some mutual funds also charge account fees. These could be for maintaining accounts with low balances, for retirement accounts, or for duplicating statements and tax forms.

In conclusion, it's not solely about the returns that a mutual fund brings, but also about the costs incurred to achieve those returns. These costs can vary significantly from one fund to another and should be carefully assessed before committing your money into any mutual fund. Therefore, understanding these costs will give you better control of your investments and will provide a realistic picture of what to expect from your funds.

Remember to read the fund prospectus carefully prior to investing. It's a legally required document that the SEC mandates must be made available to all potential investors. The prospectus contains key information on the fund's investment strategy, performance history, and associated costs, which should be analyzed meticulously.

From load fees to expense ratios, understanding these costs will reveal the true price of investing in mutual funds, which is essential for making a well-informed investment decision. After all, investments shouldn't just multiply your money but should also promote a sense of empowerment and financial literacy.

Chapter 9. Investment Strategies: The Role of Mutual Funds in Diversification

Mutual funds can play a crucial role in the diversification of your investment portfolio. To illustrate the role mutual funds play in diversification, think of the classic saying, "Don't put all your eggs in one basket." Diversification is the investment embodiment of this wisdom, and mutual funds act as a ready-made diversified basket to minimize risk and possibly increase returns.

9.1. How Mutual Funds Facilitate Diversification

Mutual funds offer an opportunity for diversification due to their inherent construct. Institutional investors pool the money of multiple investors to create a large fund. The fund managers then invest this pool of money across a wide variety of investments like stocks, bonds, commodities, real estate, or a blend thereof. Such a diversified collection of investments inherently reduces the risk associated with putting all your money into a single stock or bond.

Let's compare investing in an individual stock to investing in a mutual fund. If you invest in a single stock and it plummets due to adverse news or corporate mismanagement, you could lose a significant amount of your investment. Conversely, if you invest in a mutual fund comprising 100 companies and one of them performs poorly, its impact on your portfolio will be far less dramatic.

The diversity mutual funds offer doesn't only protect investors against losses but also presents opportunities for higher returns. When one sector does poorly, another might do well, which establishes a balance. The result is not necessarily smashing returns year after year., but rather a steadier, more predictable overall investment return.

9.2. The Math Behind Diversification

The concept of portfolio variance aids in understanding the mathematical vigour behind diversification. Consider an instance where you have invested in two stocks. The variance, or the extent of deviation that these individual stocks might have from their average return, could be significant. And higher the variance, greater the investment risk.

But when you couple these two stocks into a portfolio, the portfolio variance is not a simple average of the individual variances. Instead, it also includes the correlation of these securities, which could potentially reduce the portfolio's overall risk. This phenomenon underscores the power of diversification. And mutual funds, with their basket of stocks (or other assets), are built on this principle.

Stock	Expected Return (%)	Variance	Correlation with Others	Portfolio Variance
Stock A	6	4	0.7	3.12
Stock B	8	5	0.7	3.12

The above table presents an example demonstrating this scenario. Despite Stock A and Stock B having individual variances of 4 and 5, respectively, their combination results in a portfolio variance of just 3.12, less than either of the individual variances.

9.3. Choosing the Right Mutual Fund for Diversification

Identifying the right mutual fund mostly relies on your financial goals and risk appetite. If you're seeking potential growth and are tolerant of high risk, an equity mutual fund might be ideal. In contrast, if you want to preserve your capital and receive periodic income, a bond fund might be better suited for your needs.

A blend of both could also be an option. Balanced or hybrid mutual funds provide a single diversified package of both bonds and stocks. Such funds can balance reward and risk while giving exposure to multiple types of investments.

Fund Type	Risk Level	Ideal For
Equity Mutual Fund	High	Growth, long-term goals
Bond Mutual Fund	Low	Income, capital preservation
Balanced/Hybrid Mutual Fund	Moderate	Balanced risk-reward, multiple exposure

Choosing the right sector and geographic exposure is also essential. Mutual funds can provide exposure to different sectors (technology, healthcare, real estate, etc.) and geographical regions (country-specific, emerging markets, global, etc.). Diversity on such parameters can guard against sector-specific or region-specific turmoil.

Mutual funds allow for easy rebalancing, which is a method of keeping your portfolio's asset allocation in alignment with your investment strategy. As markets shift, your investments might drift away from your original asset allocation. Periodic portfolio rebalancing can ensure your investments align with your goals, which leads us to transaction cost efficiency.

9.4. Diversification and Transaction Cost Efficiency

Investing in a broad array of securities individually could incur significant transaction costs. Making such investments through mutual funds, however, can be more cost-efficient because it allows the investment to be pooled. Mutual funds can afford to trade large volumes at once, which reduces transaction costs per unit invested.

In conclusion, diversifying your investments to manage risk and potential return is a cornerstone of wise investing. Mutual funds can be a critical tool in this endeavor because they offer diversification built into their design. By understanding how these funds work and making mindful decisions on selecting the right funds, you can make progress towards your financial objectives while keeping risks in check. Remember, patience is a virtue here, and playing the long game could potently boost your wealth-building journey.

Chapter 10. Underlying Assets of Mutual Funds: Bonds, Stocks, and beyond

Before delving into the specifics of mutual funds, it's important to gain a foundational understanding of their building blocks: the underlying assets. Generally, these assets consist of stocks, bonds, and other types of securities. Each of them carries its unique characteristics and risk-return profiles, regardless of whether they're part of a mutual fund.

10.1. Understanding Stocks

When we talk about stocks, we are referring to equity investments, which essentially mean buying an ownership stake in a company. By purchasing shares or stocks of a company, an investor becomes a partial owner and stands to gain from the company's prosperity.

When a company performs well, its stock prices often rise, providing capital gains to the shareholders. Besides, some companies also distribute a part of their profits to shareholders in the form of dividends. However, stocks can be volatile, and their prices can fluctuate dramatically, which poses a risk of capital loss to the investor.

10.2. Delving into Bonds

Known as fixed income securities, bonds are essentially loans that investors make to the issuer, typically a corporation or a governmental body. The issuers promise to pay back the principal amount along with interest, also known as coupon payment, at specified intervals until the bond reaches its maturity date.

Bonds are often considered safer investments than stocks since the interest payments and the return of principal are contractually guaranteed unless the issuer defaults. Bonds can help to preserve capital and generate steady income. However, they usually offer a lower return compared to stocks over the long term.

10.3. Exploring Other Securities

Beyond stocks and bonds, mutual funds might hold other types of securities such as short-term debt instruments, often referred to as cash equivalents or money market instruments, and derivatives.

Cash equivalents include Treasury bills, certificates of deposit, and commercial papers. They are highly liquid and often used to park excess cash by many funds.

Derivatives are more complex financial instruments, derived from the value of underlying assets like stocks, bonds, commodities, currencies, or even interest rates. They are often used for hedging risks or for speculation.

10.4. Hybrid Assets

Some mutual funds contain a mix of stocks and bonds, or other asset classes. These hybrids aim to reduce the associated risk of investing in a single asset class, offering a balanced portfolio to investors. The assets are usually strategically allocated to align with specific objectives of the fund.

10.5. International Exposure

Further broadening the horizon, some mutual funds invest in international or global assets. Investing in foreign markets allows fund managers to take advantage of growth opportunities that might not be available domestically. However, this comes with additional risks, including currency risk and geopolitical risk.

10.6. Specialized Sectors

There are also sector-specific mutual funds that invest in particular industries such as technology, healthcare, or utilities. These funds might offer higher returns if the chosen sector performs well but carry higher risk due to the lack of diversification.

10.7. Asset Allocation

The process of spreading investments across various asset types to optimize risk and reward based on an individual's goals, risk tolerance, and investment horizon is called asset allocation. A mutual fund's goal might be to grow fast (predominantly stocks), to provide income (bonds and dividend-paying stocks), or to protect capital (bonds and cash equivalents).

In conclusion, understanding the underlying assets of a mutual fund is crucial in making informed investment decisions. These assets can significantly affect the fund's performance and risk profile. The more knowledge you, as an investor, have about these components, the better equipped you'll be to navigate through the complex, yet rewarding realm of mutual funds.

Chapter 11. Your First Investment: A Step-by-Step Guide to Buying Mutual Funds

Entering the world of investing can be intimidating at first, but once you understand the process and start investing, it becomes a journey of lifelong learning and wealth creation. In this section, we will discuss the step-by-step process of how to buy mutual funds, the time-tested vehicle for wealth accumulation.

11.1. Understanding Mutual Funds

A mutual fund is an investment vehicle that pools together money from multiple investors to invest in a diversified portfolio of stocks, bonds, or other assets. This allows individual investors to invest in a diverse range of assets which would otherwise be out of their reach due to high investment costs. The fund is managed by professional fund managers who make investment decisions based on thorough research and analysis.

11.2. Why Mutual Funds?

Mutual funds offer diversification – even with a small amount invested, you get a share in a diversified portfolio. This reduces the risk as compared to single security investments. Another advantage is professional management. Fund managers have expertise and resources to manage funds which individual investors might not possess. The ease and simplicity of investing, along with the potential for higher returns, make mutual funds a popular investment option.

11.3. How to Choose the Right Mutual Fund

Investing in mutual funds begins with figuring out your financial goals. These could be short-term (like buying a car in a couple years), medium-term (like saving for your child's education), or long-term (like retirement planning).

Once you've defined your financial goals, consider important factors like your risk tolerance, investment horizon, and expected returns. You need to match these factors to the appropriate mutual fund. For instance, equity funds might be suited for long-term goals and high risk tolerance, while debt funds might be more appropriate for short-term goals with low risk tolerance.

11.4. Open an Investment Account

To invest in mutual funds, you'll first need to open an investment account, typically with a brokerage or a mutual fund company. You can do this online, and it involves submitting a few personal details and identification documents. Some mutual funds houses also require you to complete a risk profile questionnaire.

11.5. Start Investing

Once your account is active, you can start investing. Select the mutual fund you want to invest in and decide how much you want to invest. There are two primary ways to invest in a mutual fund - lump-sum investment or systematic investment plan (SIP).

With a lump-sum investment, you invest a large amount at one go. On the other hand, with a SIP, you invest a fixed amount regularly, say each week, month, or quarter. SIPs encourage disciplined investing and are an effective way to average out your cost of investment over a period of time.

Most mutual fund companies offer online platforms where you can complete the transaction after selecting the fund and the mode of investment. Upon completion, you'll receive a confirmation with details of your purchase, including the number of mutual fund units purchased and the net asset value (NAV) at the time of purchase.

11.6. Monitor Your Investments

Once you've invested in mutual funds, it's important to regularly monitor their performance. However, do not be overly concerned with short-term fluctuations. Investing in mutual funds is a long-term endeavor, and it's the long-term performance that matters.

Remember, investing is as much about patience and discipline as it is about making the right decisions. Automated services such as SIPs make these aspects easier to manage. You can also reinvest the gains from your investments to harness the power of compound interest.

Given the dynamic nature of markets, you may need to adjust your portfolio over time according to changes in the market and in your financial goals. What matters most is staying committed to your plan.

In conclusion, investing in mutual funds isn't too complicated. With some research and careful planning, you can make mutual funds a cornerstone on your financial journey. The key is to start investing and keep learning along the way.